M000219998

ATR Publishing

Managing Your Tea Room Kitchen Effectively

Controlling Costs and Menu Planning without Sacrificing Quality

By Amy Lawrence

Published by:
ATR Publishing

Cover Photos by:
Ploy Kitjawat

Back Cover Photo by:
Sirlin Photographers
(916)444-8464
http://www.sirlin.com/

CONTENTS

INTRODUCTION

Let's face it, if you're planning a menu for a tea party of 8, it's easy. You can do all sorts of wild and exotic things that take a bit of time. But when you are planning a menu for a tea room that serves over 300 people per week or more with limited staff and a finite budget, what do you do then?

As a tea room owner for almost 7 years, I began as most tea room owners do, very excited about planning my tea room menu. I had always loved cooking and had many creative ideas. When I opened my tea room, I couldn't wait to plan the menu every week. I had big ideas for garnishes and special dishes but I soon realized that creative ideas often take time and money and those were things I didn't have much of, especially in the early days.

During that first year I also learned that what I wanted to serve wasn't always what others wanted to eat. I love mushrooms and blue cheese, but when I made dishes that contained these ingredients, I discovered that a majority of my customers did not. Over the years, by listening to my staff and customers, I gradually developed my own system and guidelines for creating tea room menus and managing my tea room kitchen. It is my hope that this book will give you many creative ideas and you find it useful for your own tea room. Best of luck!

-Amy

CHAPTER 1

Designing Your Tea Room Menu

Food plays an important role in your tea room. It helps to enhance and imprint in the mind those special memories with friends and loved ones. Your menu should be fantastic! Customers come to your tea room to get away and be pampered. You want to make their experience one they won't soon forget. Not only do you want customers looking forward to coming to your tea room, but you also want them to visit often. If you do the same menu week after week and there's no variety, your customers will get bored and end up going somewhere else. One of the goals of your tea room should be to keep your customers coming back on a regular basis and bring in new friends to share the experience.

There are 5 key points to remember when designing your menu.

Use quality ingredients

Make the most of that one bite. Tea foods are tiny. Every bite counts so make the most of it! Don't try and skimp by using artificial vanilla, and other cheaper ingredients. If you want to set yourself apart and be the best, use the best ingredients.

Use simple recipes

Remember the number of guests – the more guests, the more work. Be mindful of this. Our first Valentine's Day, we decided to make cute little egg salad sandwiches. We thought it would be great to cut them in heart shapes and then garnish with a smaller heart cut out of bread on top. This sounded like a wonderful idea at the time. Later we realized that meant 3 hearts were needed for each sandwich. This is fine if you have 8 people. 8 people means cutting 24 hearts, but 100 people means 300 hearts. See the problem? Keep the number of guests in mind at all times!

Think about color

When planning your tea menu, think about the color of your foods. Use a variety of breads – dill rye, dark rye, buttermilk, white, wheat all work well. Make sure all of your desserts aren't the same color. Variety is the key! Make sure they are different colors and not all beige. (A dessert plate of apple cobbler, sugar cookie, and oatmeal bar equals boring!)

Think about shape

Use a different shape or look for each sandwich – open-faced, closed, cut out, etc. Choose different garnishes for each one. This goes for desserts too. Have a dessert in a dish, a bar cookie and a round cookie. Mix it up!

While the shapes are good, the colors are too similar.

Don't use the same ingredient in everything

This is especially true with nuts, garlic, seafood and fruit. Think about your guests' tastes and possible allergies. Unless you know them extremely well, plan your menu around someone not liking a certain ingredient. For example, if you use pecans in the Jamaican Banana Scone, don't use nuts in the other scone. If you are using cinnamon, don't use it in all of your desserts. This avoids many potential problems. You can easily give a customer 2 of the same dessert if for some reason they can't eat one of them, but if they all contain the same ingredients, you're out of luck.

In our tea room, we offered 3 menu options:

1. The full afternoon tea which included: 1 slice of our famous Black Forest Quiche, a cup of soup/salad, depending on the season, 3 tea sandwiches, one with meat, the other two veggie, and 2 scones.

2. The light afternoon tea included the tea tray but did not include the quiche or soup/salad.
3. Cream tea which included: 2 scones, lemon curd and Devonshire and a pot of tea.

Our Black Forest Quiche was our signature dish. This never changed and was always available with the full afternoon tea (although we did offer a vegetarian option). During the fall and winter we served soup in a tea cup and in the spring and summer it was a small salad served in the tea cup.

CHAPTER 2

Rotating Your Menu on a Schedule

By rotating some of your menu items on a schedule, you can provide variety to your customers while also controlling your costs. As mentioned before, providing variety is important as it keeps your customers returning. Our tea room was known for its delicious food and our customers came in regularly wanting new items. We developed a system that put our menu items on a rotating schedule, that way we weren't always making entirely new recipes every week. It wasn't a hard and fast rotation but a guideline. Generally speaking, we kept our sandwich and dessert recipes for about 3 weeks at a time. Every week we changed one or two items on the menu. For example, if this week we made Sesame Chicken Sandwiches, Sundried Tomato Sandwich and Easy Cucumber, the next week we would change one sandwich and one dessert to something else. That way if a customer came in again the following week, they would have at least one new sandwich and one new dessert on the menu. Following these guidelines meant that every 3 weeks the menu was totally different. This 3 week menu rotation worked extremely well for our menu planning and kitchen work load and it pleased our customers who visited frequently.

We phased sandwiches in and out depending on our ingredients on hand. If we had a lot of sundried tomato spread left over, then next week we would continue that sandwich. We frequently used a cream cheese base sandwich with various fresh herbs as they could often carry over to the next week. They actually tasted even better the following week after all the flavors blended together. We paid close attention to food spoilage guidelines so any sandwich fillings with meat would not be used the next week. If we used the same chicken tea sandwich recipe the next week, we would make a new batch using fresh ingredients.

We found it important to have a few signature dishes, otherwise customers were disappointed if we didn't have a few of their favorites. This also provided consistency to our menu. By far, our Black Forest Ham Quiche was one of our signature dishes. We made 48 quiche at a time, baked them entirely, cooled and then froze them. Late in the afternoon, we would take as many quiche as needed and put in the refrigerator for the next day's reservations always adding a few extras in the count for walk-ins.

The soup we made fresh weekly but only changed the soup recipe a few times during the season.

Scones were made fresh daily, the kinds of scones made depended on the fruit in season. Any leftovers were used the next day or frozen for an emergency supply.

CHAPTER 3

Weekly Menu Planning and Grocery Shopping

It's important to plan your menu weekly. I met with my staff every Friday to go over the menu for the next week and plan the grocery shopping list. Weekly planning helps you control your costs by using ingredients you already have and not allow them to go to waste. By making templates of your menu planning sheet and shopping list, you save time and energy. It's also great to organize your grocery list by the layout of the stores that you use. This makes for quicker shopping especially if you have to send someone new to the store that may not be familiar with the layout. Also it is handy to have a white board hanging in your kitchen, staff can add needed items to the board daily which you can add later to your weekly list.

Here's an example of our Menu Planning Sheet. It's also nice to have this sheet when your cook is absent or when you have staff changes over the weekend so everyone knows what to do.

Afternoon to Remember's Menu and Instructions of the Week Date:_____

Scones _____and _____Salad _____
Dressing _____Topping _____

Sandwiches:

1. _____Bread _____Shape _____Garnish _____
2. _____Bread _____Shape _____Garnish _____
3. _____Bread _____Shape _____Garnish _____

Desserts:

1. _____Dish/Cut _____Garnish/Topping _____
2. _____Dish/Cut _____Garnish/Topping _____
3. _____Dish/Cut _____Garnish/Topping _____

Special Instructions:

☐ 1. Quiche – Take out of freezer and put in refrigerator.
☐ 2. Make up sandwiches.
☐ 3. Dish out desserts.
☐ 4. Dish out lemon curd/Devonshire.
☐ 5. Write up board for next day.
☐ _____
☐ _____

Example of Afternoon to Remember's partial shopping list:

Sam's Club	WinCo
☐ Flowers x ___	☐ Buttermilk x ___
☐ Cream Cheese x ___	☐ Spinach x ___
☐ Milk x ___	
☐ Sour Cream x ___	☐ Dill Bread x ___
☐ Whipping Cream x ___	☐ Wheat x ___
☐ Eggs x ___	☐ Dark Rye x ___
☐ Butter x ___	☐ 5 Seed x ___
☐ Parmesan 3 Cheese x ___	☐ Cake Mix x ___
☐ Cheddar x ___	☐ White Chocolate x ___
☐ Chicken x ___	☐ Toffee Chips x ___
	☐ Lime Juice x ___
☐ Cucumber x ___	☐ Coconut x ___
☐ Tomatoes x ___	☐ Sweetened Condensed x ___
☐ Onions x ___	
☐ Garlic x ___	☐ Pudding x ___
☐ Lemons x ___	☐ Spices x ___
☐ Fruit for scones x ___	
	☐ Dried Oregano x ___
☐ Dried Fruit x ___	☐ Dried Basil x ___
☐ Pecans x ___	☐ Dry Mustard x ___
☐ Walnuts x ___	☐ Poppy Seeds x ___
☐ Sliced Almonds x ___	☐ Dill Weed x ___
	☐ Dill Seed x ___
☐ Buttermilk Bread x ___	
☐ Potato Bread x ___	☐ Sundried Tomatoes x ___
☐ Mayo x ___	☐ Candy x ___
☐ Canola Oil x ___	
☐ Canned Tomatoes x ___	
☐ Maraschino Cherry x ___	
☐ Canned Apricots x ___	
☐ Mandarins x ___	
☐ Olive Oil x ___	
...	

Ordering Supplies

With my tea room we ordered the main staples such as flour, eggs, and pie shells from a restaurant supply company (Sysco) about every 2-3 weeks, but we still needed items from our local stores. We were very fortunate to be able to buy much of our produce from our local market, which was within walking distance of our tea room.

I also discovered, "Click and Pull" from Sam's Club and I'm sure Costco has something similar. This saved me an incredible amount of time. You order the items ahead of time online and pick them up at a scheduled time in the future. It was a wonderful time saver!

CHAPTER 4

Foods to Avoid on Your Menu

This is not an absolute list and it depends on your customer's tastes, but in our tea room we found that menu items with these ingredients were most often left on the plate or asked to be substituted:

- Mushrooms
- Blue cheese
- Onions (we did use these quite frequently but made sure not every sandwich included them)
- Red and green peppers (again, we did use these, but made sure not every sandwich had them)
- Seafood (we saved this for special occasions in a buffet setting)

CHAPTER 5

When Should You Change Your Prices?

Unfortunately I learned the hard way about changing my prices. I recommend you do a cost analysis no less than one time per year. This allows you to determine if your prices are adequate. It is a pain to do and can take a lot of time the first time you do it, but the results are well worth it. One of my biggest mistakes was not raising prices for 3 years. When I finally redid my cost analysis, I found I needed to raise my afternoon teas by $2.00. I can't tell you how many complaints I had when I did that. Every year after that, I raised my prices just a little and always during the holiday season when it wasn't so noticeable. If you do not raise prices every year, then when you do make a large price change, it will be a big deal to your customers.

CHAPTER 6

Should You Offer Vegetarian, Gluten-Free and Other Special Menus?

My advice on special menus, is to try it and see. Every tea room and location is different. We didn't have enough of the special diet customers to find it worthwhile to have a separate menu. We tried accommodating special dietary needs but with the exception of the vegetarian choices, we found that it was very expensive to maintain. Because we made everything from scratch, we tried accommodating diabetics by making sugar-free scones and desserts but often those customers who requested a special diet often did not show up for their reservation. The amount of time, effort and extra grocery shopping for that one person was wasted as the chances of another walk-in customer having those same dietary requirements the same day was very small. However to accommodate those customers with special dietary requirements, we allowed them to bring in their own food and we would plate it for them. This allowed the customer to dine with her guests and it saved us from many headaches and expenses.

If you decide that you want to do vegan, gluten-free, sugar-free and other special diets, be sure and advertise that fact. I'm sure with the proper marketing you will become "the" tea place to visit among those special diet populations.

One very important note, remember that it's okay to say, "No!" It's your tea room, you can't please everyone all of the time. If it's too much for you to do special diets and offering 3 afternoon teas is all you can handle, that's okay. Just do those three teas the very best you can and provide the best customer service you possibly can. Often times we think we need to be able to do it all and offer it all. Specialize in what you do best!

CHAPTER 7

Controlling Costs without Sacrificing Quality

It's so important to be on top of your food costs when owning a tea room. In the restaurant industry the average of food costs is about 30% compared to the total operating budget. Depending on your tea room model, it can be much less. My food costs were extremely low – around 20%. This was due to these factors:

- Our tea room was mainly by reservation, this helped us know exactly how much food to prepare, we did allow walk-ins but only when there was space available and food on hand
- The menu items were fixed this meant that we did not need to have ingredients on-hand that were used infrequently
- Yearly cost analysis of various menu items
- Rotating our menu according to ingredients on hand, foods in season, limiting our recipes to more simple ones to prepare
- Freezing items individually so we could use them by piece (such as quiche)

Doing a cost analysis of your menu items is critical to the success of your business. It definitely takes a lot of time, but the results are well worth it. It's important to include your staff in the cost analysis process so they understand the importance of portion control and can help with the menu planning in order to keep your costs down.

When doing a cost analysis, it's important to be as accurate as you possibly can. You may have to "guess" on a few things, but the more you do your research and use exact numbers the better your analysis will be.

Here's an example of a cost analysis of our famous quiche:

Cost	Ingredient
$340.00	Black Forest ham and Jarlsberg cheese from our local cheese shop
$5.00	Onions
$52.00	pie shells (48)
$3.00	Eggs
$5.00	Milk
$20.00	Whipping Cream
$5.00	Flour and Foil (estimate)
$60.00	4 hours of prep time labor cost of $15 per hour
Total cost: $490.00 $10.21 for each quiche (48 quiche) $.85 per slice (12 slices per quiche)	

This does not include cost to run the oven, but it's a pretty close estimate.

You should do this for every type of item you offer on your menu. Since this is a long process, I always did a representative sample. I tried to pick the most expensive items that I made and that way I knew the top price for each item. For example, when determining scone prices, I would do an analysis on the scone recipe that had the highest ingredient costs – such as a recipe with dried cherries. Then I would know that all of the other scones would fall at or below that cost. I would do this for the quiche, chicken sandwich, salad with homemade dressing, soup, scones with fruit and one dessert which included chocolate and nuts. By basing my analysis on these items, I knew when I chose the next week's menu I would be at or under those costs.

When you do a cost analysis, make sure you write down exactly how much time it took to prepare the dish, the amount of ingredients you used and how much it made. That way the next time you do a cost analysis, you can just substitute the new costs for ingredients and labor and not have to recreate everything from scratch.

Here's an example of a cost analysis menu:

Cost	Menu Item
$1.17	One cup of salad with home-made dressing
$.85	Slice of quiche
$.55 x 3	3 Tea Sandwiches
$.35 x 3	3 Desserts
$.35 x 2	2 Scones (I based price on fresh fruit scone)
$.27	Pot of tea
Total Menu Cost: $5.69 per person (this does not include lemon curd, Devonshire, waitress service, napkins, kitchen clean up).	

Our menu price for the full afternoon tea was $24.95.

When determining your menu cost, you should look at the prices of other tea rooms in the area as well as the cost of rent. There is a restaurant formula for determining menu prices. You take the total cost of food and divide by .35 giving you a menu price. Using this formula, our total cost is $5.69/.35=$16.26 menu price. However, this is a restaurant formula and there are some important differences between a restaurant and a tea room. Making and garnishing tea sandwiches takes considerably more time than putting together a mass-produced dish. Restaurants also turn tables around quickly while afternoon tea is an experience and as such, customers stay for a longer period of time. Base your menu price from your cost analysis, the going rates of afternoon tea in your area, labor costs, rent as well as your own good judgment.

CHAPTER 8

Ideas to Help You Control Costs

Ice cream scoops

Certain items can help you control costs in your tea room. Using ice cream scoops can not only make it easier to put sandwich filling on bread slices, but it also helps you control the amount of filling you use. When doing your cost analysis, you can determine exactly how many sandwiches you can make in a batch by measuring out how many scoops of filling you have. It keeps everything consistent when making sandwiches as well. This in turn helps with your customer image as all sandwiches are "the same." Customers know exactly what to expect every time they come in for tea. Ice cream scoops work well for scoopable desserts such as cobblers and pudding as well as for Devonshire and Lemon Curd.

Doubling and Tripling Recipes

Although it may not seem like such a time-saving idea at first, but by writing down your measurements when you double and triple a recipe, you save lots of time. It also prevents mistakes in measuring when you write out your large recipes. This was one of those ideas that took me a while to realize how much time I spent when I tripled my quiche recipe. I mentally did the calculation every time I made a batch of 48 quiches. One day I decided to actually write down the large recipe. Wow! I couldn't believe how much time I had been wasting every time I made quiche. I did this for all of our recipes and decided to publish them in our book, "Master Tea Room Recipes".

Clean out your refrigerator and freezer on a weekly basis

If you clean out your refrigerator and freezer once a week at the end of the week, you won't let expensive food go to waste. This will help you will know what you have and what you need to buy. We often did this on Friday afternoons before we had our menu planning/shopping list meeting. That way if we had too much of one ingredient, we could plan our menu so that it included that ingredient.

Put Recipes in Clear Plastic Sleeves

Try putting your recipes in clear plastic sleeves and putting them in a 3 ring binder. This keeps them from getting dirty and "getting lost," which can happen easily in a tea room kitchen. You also gain points with your health department inspector as well as the recipes can easily be wiped clean.

CHAPTER 9

The Value of Using Check Off Lists

I can't stress to you enough the importance of check off lists. Having a check off list saves you lots of time, money and frustration. They take some time in the beginning to set up, but after they are done, they are invaluable. Here's why:

1. Everyone knows what to do. The job is stated in writing. It can be checked off. There is little miscommunication.
2. It's an excellent tool for training purposes. Employees can refer to the list if they are confused about what to do.
3. It provides consistency.
4. They are great when you are tired. You don't even have to think, just follow the list and you won't forget to do something important.
5. They save you lots of time; it's easier to delegate when you are going off to an event. Just give someone your event check off sheet, they can pack up all of the supplies for you and you'll have everything you need.

I used check off lists for everything. I had kitchen morning check lists, closing lists, tea room prep lists, cleaning lists, shopping lists and inventory lists.

By using a check off sheet, you don't specifically have to assign jobs. Staff can complete tasks and return to the list and check them off and choose another job. By checking off they completed the task, they have indicated to others that job is done. This prevents duplication and the need to tell someone, "it's already done," If the manager is on the phone, or busy in the kitchen, the staff member doesn't need to ask someone what to do.

Checks off lists are also perfect when you are doing events, especially if you are taking your items elsewhere. By using them, you won't forget the important items such as business cards and mailing signup sheets. You won't have to recreate the wheel every time you do an event, just print it out, pack and you're ready to go.

In addition they are great for accountability – especially with closing lists. Have staff members initial when they complete the list. If something doesn't get done you know who to talk to and who is responsible.

You can have check off lists for morning prep, afternoon prep, once a week cleaning schedule, closing schedule etc. Once the list is created, just save it and print it out as needed.

In the following pages, I give you some of my examples. These are specialized to our tea room, but you can create your own.

Daily Morning Check List

- ☐ Start hot water machines.
- ☐ Fill water pitchers.
- ☐ Copy daily schedule and check against board for any changes
- ☐ Make reset boxes if necessary.
- ☐ Put out outdoor accessories.
- ☐ Water plants. Must be watered in morning, not evening.
- ☐ Vacuum
- ☐ Print out new menus if needed.
- ☐ Write names on menu signs.
- ☐ Check all table settings for the day including napkins.
- ☐ Place menus on each place setting.
- ☐ Fill sugar and cookie jars.
- ☐ Cut lemons for water.
- ☐ Get tea socks.
- ☐ Fill tea canisters if needed.
- ☐ Fold napkins.
- ☐ Empty trash cans in office/front counter/bathroom/prep
- ☐ Clean bathroom – empty trash, clean sink, toilet & mirror
- ☐ Put paper towels/toilet paper in bathrooms.
- ☐ Check for thank you packets, make up if needed.
- ☐ Put out guest checks and tea order forms.
- ☐ Clean glass on front door.
- ☐ Clean out window sills – look for flies
- ☐ Start sample pot
- ☐ Put out lemon curd and Devonshire cream
- ☐ Turn on fountain in garden room and all lamps and lights.
- ☐ Turn on music
- ☐ Check to see if we have enough to-go boxes
- ☐ Check flowers on tables

Daily Kitchen Extended Check List

Morning Open -11:00

- ☐ Put soup on
- ☐ Cut sandwiches
- ☐ Plate
- ☐ Lemon Curd/Devonshire
- ☐ Cut quiche
- ☐ Glaze scones
- ☐ Quiche plates
- ☐ Fill milk pitchers
- ☐ Flower bucket/water
- ☐ Make up sanitizer water
- ☐ Take butter, cream cheese out of refrigerator
- ☐ Take cookies out if any
- ☐ Keep counters, workspace clean
- ☐ Combine scones

Afternoon 12:00-1:00

- ☐ Make sandwiches for next day
- ☐ Make dessert for next day
- ☐ Lemon Curd/Devonshire
- ☐ Quiche Plates
- ☐ Wipe down counters
- ☐ Change sanitizer water
- ☐ Change/takeout flowers/water
- ☐ Check soup for 1:00
- ☐ Sweep kitchen periodically

Afternoon 1:00-Closing

- ☐ Lemon Curd/Devonshire
- ☐ Quiche Plates

- ☐ Wipe down counters
- ☐ Change sanitizer water
- ☐ Change water for flowers and put away
- ☐ Check soup for 3:00
- ☐ Organize shelves
- ☐ Put plates above soup area
- ☐ Clean under pot holders
- ☐ Clean dishwasher
- ☐ Lemon Curd/Devonshire-make at end of day for next day
- ☐ Make Lemon/Curd Devonshire -to go's
- ☐ Combine scones
- ☐ Fill self-rising flour, regular flour, sugar
- ☐ Take out quiche for next day
- ☐ Make tags; do board
- ☐ Sweep, mop-final
- ☐ Clean scone rack
- ☐ Organize back room
- ☐ Clean microwave
- ☐ Wipe down refrigerators
- ☐ Clean sinks
- ☐ Take/change garbage out
- ☐ Cover anything that needs to be in refrigerator
- ☐ Fill paper towels
- ☐ Fold laundry
- ☐ Wrap scones
- ☐ Clean dish buckets, silverware container and bleach bucket
- ☐ Make scone bowls for next day

<u>Daily Kitchen Closing List and Check Off Sheet</u>

☐ Empty and rinse out tea socks.

☐ Wash all dishes including baking sheets.

☐ Put all dishes away.

☐ Wipe down all counter tops.

☐ Scrub sinks with 409 cleaner

☐ Wipe out microwave.

☐ Wipe out refrigerator and freezer on Saturday.

☐ Cover all items in refrigerator.

☐ All left overs on Sunday need to be cleaned out.

☐ Sweep and mop under all tables.

☐ Clean behind air conditioners and wipe off air conditioners

☐ Wash carts and legs including baker's rack.

☐ Clean refrigerator and microwave fronts

☐ Fill self-rising flour and sugar bins

☐ Clean drains on Sunday

☐ Take out trash, empty kitchen, bathroom and tea prep areas

☐ Wipe down walls and doorways using bleach water

☐ Wipe off table shelves

Amy wants everything nice and sparkling clean! ☺

CHAPTER 10

Easy Garnishes in a Hurry

As most tea room owners know, garnishing the tea sandwiches is often what takes the time. Unfortunately they can't be done too far in advance. If you garnish the day before, the sandwiches look lifeless and not fresh. My staff and I came up with some easy and quick garnishes to do the day of the event. One thing to remember is that individually they might not need to have an elaborate garnish, as collectively they look beautiful together on a tray.

Here are some easy garnishes that add a bit of pizzazz but don't take much time to do:

Sandwich Garnishes

Often time by using different colored breads and different shaped sandwiches you can vary the appearance on the tray – squares, fingers, triangles and you don't even need a garnish but for garnish ideas try these:

Variety is key

- Dried parsley mixed with sesame seeds/basil/lemon zest – sprinkle on edges of chicken salad tea sandwiches
- Pecan halves – just place one on an open-faced sandwich
- Olive slice – just place one green or black or both on an open-faced sandwich, sprinkle with appropriate spice, such as paprika or seasoning salt
- Cucumber – thinly sliced, thickly sliced, diced, quartered, or triangle pieces, sprinkle with lemon pepper
- Lemon pepper adds a little something when sprinkled over an open faced sandwich
- Seasoning salt – same idea as above

Simple garnishes look elegant when put together

- Flat parsley leaf – these can take a bit of time if you let them, but just place one leaf on an open-faced sandwich
- Tomato with dried basil sprinkled on top

Dessert Garnishes

- If you use whipped cream on your dessert, try and sprinkle a little cocoa, turbinado sugar, cinnamon, or lemon zest curls on top to make it really pop!

- Drizzle – use melted white or dark/semisweet chocolate and "drizzle" it over dessert bars, cookies, and cakes. It adds a bit of pizzazz without you spending too much time frosting the entire dessert. During the holiday season, try drizzling white chocolate over cookies and then adding crushed peppermint candies.
- Dip ½ cookie in melted white chocolate

- Use a raspberry or blueberry and place in a small amount of frosting or whipped cream
- Chocolate pieces, white or dark
- Powdered sugar
- Lemon curls
- Turbinado sugar sprinkled on cookies while baking
- Try placing a nut half standing up

I try and use whatever is in the dish to garnish. If it's a dish with cherries, then I might place a dried cherry on top. If it's chocolate dessert, then maybe a chocolate chip on top.

CHAPTER 11

Tips and Tricks to Making, Storing, and Serving Large Quantities of Food

When you serve large quantities of people, the ability to store your food efficiently is a must. It's much easier to prepare a large batch and have a few leftovers vs. having to remake another batch of something at the last minute. Therefore, it's important to invest in a large freezer and a good refrigerator at the beginning. Unfortunately this is one of the lessons I learned the  hard way early on. If I opened another tea room today, I would buy new appliances – the biggest freezer and refrigerator I could afford. I suggest the biggest you can afford because refrigerator and freezer space were always a constant battle in my tea room. After purchasing used equipment, I spent more in repairs than it would have cost to purchase the equipment new. In addition, the stress I endured when these items quit working plus the headaches of lost food was definitely worth the cost of new equipment. Due to tax reasons, leasing your equipment may be a better option for you and you should consult with your accountant about it. Having great and reliable equipment is one of the keys to your success. By using new equipment you will save yourself tons of money and headaches.

Frozen vs. Fresh

In my tea room, we prided ourselves on our homemade food. Having fresh items were very important to me. I was a stickler on scones made fresh daily and cookies baked daily. However, I also realized the importance of freezing in order to save time. There were some items which were fine to freeze and some definitely not. Quiche, cookie dough, soup bases, bread all freeze quite well. Sandwich fillings do not.

Once your tea room has been up and running for a few months, you will begin to learn the amount of food and preparation required every week. You will learn what you can and can't freeze. You will develop your own system and decide what works best for you.

Cooking Schedule

Our tea room offered tea service Wednesday through Sunday. Tuesday was our biggest prep day of the week. My cooks would come in and prepare much of the food needed for the entire week. All of the fillings would be made on this day as well as the desserts, lemon curd, and Devonshire Cream. Every afternoon they would make up the sandwiches for the next day. In the morning, they would come in make scones, cut and garnish the sandwiches, put the soup on or prepare salad and plate the trays. Depending how busy our weekends were, usually on Friday, they often needed to make more chicken sandwich filling and maybe one or two desserts.

We learned that we needed to make 48 quiche about every 2 weeks. Depending on the season, the cooks would come in on Monday if it were during the holiday season or very early on Tuesday to make the quiche. Because the quiche were quite a bit of work and took a lot of oven time, we found it beneficial to make them in large batches. It was definitely an assembly line process. Given the amount of prep time and how the process scaled, it was practically just as easy to make 48 as it was 12. After they were all baked, we wrapped each quiche carefully in foil and froze them. We would thaw out the required number of quiche we needed the night before in the refrigerator. Before reheating them, we cut them into 12 slices. Cutting is easier when the quiche were cold and the slices look much neater than cutting them after reheating. Because we didn't use as many vegetarian quiche per week, we would bake only a few vegetarian quiche at a time, cool them, cut them and freeze each slice individually. That way, when a customer requested vegetarian, we wouldn't have to thaw out an entire quiche.

Freezing also works well for cookies.

It's so much easier to make a huge triple batch of cookies, form them into balls and place them on a cookie sheet and "flash freeze them". After flash freezing, place them in plastic bags and store in the freezer. In the morning before your customers arrive, you can bake the amount needed plus a few extra for walk-ins. It makes your tea room smell delicious and your customers always have fresh cookies.

Storing Items in Large Containers

Storing items in large clear plastic containers with lids is a great time saver. For example, if you use a lot of toasted chopped nuts, prepare a large batch and store them in an airtight container. This saves you time down the road. When you need them, they are all ready to go.

The other reason for storing them in clear containers is that you can see how much you have without opening the lid. We stored all of our flour, sugar, nuts, chocolate chips, etc in this way.

Baker's Racks

Baker's racks are a must especially when counter top space is limited. You can usually find a new one for $100 or less. Invest in at least one, possibly two racks with wheels so you can move them around, as you need space. Not only do these hold hot baking pans, but also they are great for storing scones, baked desserts that do not require refrigeration and can even hold sandwich trays while you are getting the trays prepped in the morning. You can also use it to store extra baking pans when not in use.

Making and Storing Tea Sandwiches

As a tea room owner, you want your tea sandwiches to be the freshest tasting as possible but when you have 200 people to plan for, this isn't always easy to do the morning of the event. Here are a few tricks to ease your preparation without sacrificing freshness.

Make your sandwich fillings ahead of time

Sandwich fillings can be made at least 3 days ahead. As explained earlier, most of our cream cheese filling sandwiches that include fresh herbs, actually taste better when they are made ahead of time. This gives the herbs a chance to set in. Depending on the ingredients, cream cheese fillings can last up to 2 weeks. Fillings with meat, such as chicken or ham, should be used within 5 days.

Make up your sandwiches the day before serving them

This is probably the most important tip when making sandwiches. For perfect edges, make your sandwiches the day before and cut them the day you serve them. The filling will be cold and solidified and the sandwiches will slice nicely. If you do make and cut them the same day, it's hard to get a "clean" edge.

Wrap your sandwiches carefully

Over the years we perfected the way we store our tea sandwiches. In the beginning we tried storing them in plastic containers, but found that it was difficult to keep getting into them without mangling the sandwiches. Here's the system we developed:

1. First place a sheet of parchment down on a plastic tray.

2. Lay your bread slices out on the tray, butter slices, top with filling (use an ice cream scoop for portion control and ease), top with second slice if closed sandwich.

3. Cover with a second piece of parchment paper.

4. Place one more layer of sandwiches top, never layer more than 2 layers.
5. Cover second layer with parchment paper.
6. Lightly dampen paper towels and cover parchment paper completely.

7. Wrap entire tray with plastic wrap. If you need to be able to stack trays, place another tray upside down on top of sandwiches and wrap in plastic together.

8. On the morning you are to serve the sandwiches, uncover and save the parchment paper and paper towels.
9. Cut each sandwich into tea sandwiches and garnish.
10. Lightly cover sandwiches with dampened paper towels and store in refrigerator until ready to plate. Always keep them covered as they dry out very quickly.

At our tea room, we plated our sandwiches and desserts in the morning. We set all the plates out on the counter and put the required number of sandwiches on each plate. Then we covered with a lightly dampened paper towel and stored the plates in the refrigerator until ready to serve. When an order came in, the cook placed the scones in the oven, pulled out the plate of sandwiches and desserts and put them on the 3 tiered trays. When the waitress was ready for the order she took the paper towel off of the sandwiches, made sure the hot scones were on the tray and took it all to the table.

Making and Storing Scones

I experimented with many ways to bake and store scones. I tried making them and freezing the dough, baking them halfway and freezing them, making them, baking them and then freezing. After all of this experimentation, in the end I decided that it's just best to make them the day you serve them. If you do have left overs, wrap them tightly in plastic wrap, and reheat them the next day. If you have lots of extra scones for some reason one day, then put them in a plastic container and freeze them for emergency use.

If you do make scones every day, like we did, here are a few tips to make it easier. Measure out your flour, sugar and dry ingredients the day before. When you arrive in the morning, you're all ready to go. You just add the fruit, butter, buttermilk and bake. (For extra scone tips using our recipes, see our Master Tea Room Recipe Cookbook Chapter 5.)

CHAPTER 12

The Logistics of Running a Tea Room Kitchen

Every owner has their own way of managing and running their tea room and kitchen. This is something that really can't be taught in a book but must be worked out over time. It is largely dependent on the number of staff, number of customers served and the preferences of the owner. In the beginning timing is always the hardest part. The orders needed to be taken in a timely fashion and passed along to the kitchen, the tea needs to be made and served before the food and the tea tray needs to come out hot. When customers are finished, dishes need to be bused, tables cleaned and reset and everyone needs to be ready for the next seating or next customer.

If timing isn't perfect, customers complain about wait time, cold food and poor service, this leads to staff members becoming agitated at one another and your life as a tea room owner becomes stressful and chaotic. If you want your life and tea room to be happy, then having your tea room run like clockwork is key.

I can tell you after almost 7 years of running a tea room, we finally developed our tea room into a well-oiled machine – the result of a lot of hard work and heartache. The key to running a great tea room and kitchen is communication and staff collaboration. Weekly meetings with staff to iron out problems and concerns worked well. Having an established system and way of doing things was also key.

Although everyone's tea room is different, I will explain how this system worked well for our circumstances. We were mainly a reservations based tea room. We served tea Wednesday-Saturday at 11:00, 1:00, and 3:00. On Sunday our seating times were 12:00 and 2:00. We did take walk-ins but on a case-by-case basis as space and food were available. Customers would call and make a reservation and we would put them in the reservation book and assign them a table which was labeled by letter. Toward the middle of the afternoon of each day, we would give the cook the number of reservations for the next day. She would then make up the required sandwiches and dish out the desserts. She would write all reservations on a board in the kitchen according to each seating. That way she knew how many trays to make up with the correct number of food items. This would also give her an idea of how many scones to make for the next day and how many quiche to take out and put in the refrigerator. In the morning, the waitresses would re-check the reservation book and make changes to the board. Often times there would be cancellations as well as additions.

Diagram board:

```
11:00

Table A – Susan 3F (meaning 3 full afternoon teas)
Table B – Jane 2L (meaning 2 light afternoon teas)
Table C – Mary 3F 3L

1:00

Table A – Theresa 1 F
Table B – Pat 10 F
Table C – Angela 8 L

3:00

Table A – Sharon 5 F 1 L
Table D – Nancy 1 C

Total:  22 Full, 14 Light, 1 Cream Tea
```

In addition the kitchen staff would make up sticky notes with the time of reservation and name of party to place on each 3 tier. For example: Table A Susan 5 full, 1 light; meaning 5 full teas and 1 light tea. She would put all of these sticky notes stacked with the correct number of plates needed.

In the morning, all of the dessert plates would be set out with the sticky notes indicating how many desserts to put on each plate. The same would be done for the sandwiches. Then after everything was plated, sandwiches were covered and placed back into refrigerator. Depending on the desserts, often time they were set out on the 3 tier trays on a separate table unless they needed to be refrigerated.

When a customer came in, we already knew if they wanted the full or light tea. They could always change if they wanted but usually they kept to the choice they made when the reservation was taken. When the customer arrived, the waitress took their tea order, then placed a small sticky note on the oven with the name, table letter and the number in the party. This signaled to the staff that it was time to put the scones in the oven. While the scones were reheating, generally 3 minutes or so, the kitchen staff would take out the correct tray and place it on the prep table. After the waitress took out the tea to the customer, she would return to the kitchen to pick up the tray. If the customer had ordered a full afternoon tea, the waitress would first pick up the quiche and take it to the customer. After a certain time had elapsed, she would pick up the dirty quiche dishes, return to kitchen, and put another sticky note on the oven to signal to the kitchen it was time to put in the scone order.

I realize this may sound very detailed and complicated but I had a staff of 15. On busy days we may have 10 people working at the tea room at one time. It was critical that everyone knew what was going on and was right on track. Some cooks are probably great with the waitresses shouting orders at them, but my cooks were older and liked to have things written down. We often had over 120 customers having tea, so it was critical that food get to them on time. If they did not eat on time, dishes were not returned and washed on time and the next seating wasn't ready for the next set of customers. If 11:00 ran super late, that could affect all of the seatings for the day. Therefore the tea room needed to run like clockwork at every seating.

The way you set up your tea room will most likely be totally different from ours. This was just an example so you could see how important it is to have a good and well thought out system. It doesn't matter exactly what you do as long as you create a system that works well for you. You probably will change and adapt it many times over the years but having a set system leads to happy customers and happy staff.

CHAPTER 13

Presenting the Tea Tray

I never realized how important it is to me to have the tea tray, "presented," until I visited other tea rooms that do not do this. In our tea room the waitresses would bring out the tea tray, point to specific menu items and say, "Today we have 2 kinds of freshly baked scones: Jamaican Banana Scones and our famous, Anniversary Scones. On the sandwich layer we have, Caesar Chicken Tea Sandwiches, Sun Dried Tomato Sandwiches and our classic Cucumber Sandwiches. And for the finale, we have on the dessert tray, Margarita Lime Pie, Chocolate Oatmeal Delights and a Chocolate Snap Cookie. Enjoy your tea!"

It does make a difference in how you present the food. If a waitress just comes by and "plops" the tray on the table, all of the extra things and the special attention you paid to the details just doesn't get appreciated and noticed. Make sure you deliver the tray with style! You've gone to all of that work to make everything special, be sure to finish it off in the same way. It's also a great way to point out the freshness, the use of local produce and the talents of your staff. This is your time to shine and show off your hard work! Make the most of it!

The presentation of the tray enhances the afternoon tea experience

CHAPTER 14

Should You Have a Printed Menu?

This is really a matter of preference and how much staff and resources you have. Some tea rooms just put the basics on their menu. For example:

Full Afternoon Tea:

1 slice of our famous Black Forest Quiche
1 cup of soup/salad
2 freshly baked scones
3 delicious tea sandwiches
3 gourmet tea desserts

$24.95 each

As stated before, in my tea room we offered 3 different options. The customers chose their tea option when they called in their reservation.

On our menu we did print out the 3 options and put in the names of the items we were serving for the week.

Our menu looked more like this:

Afternoon Tea Selection

~Full Afternoon Tea~

Black Forest Ham Quiche* and Tomato Basil Bisque*
Jamaican Banana Scone** and Mandarin Scone

Tea Sandwiches

Sesame Chicken, Swiss Cheese and Bacon
Artichoke with Cheese****

Desserts

White Chocolate Raspberry Cookie, Blackberry Cobbler
Chocolate Oatmeal Delight Bar*

$24.95

~Light Afternoon Tea~

Jamaican Banana Scone** and Mandarin Scone

Tea Sandwiches

Hot and Honey Chicken, Swiss Cheese and Bacon

Artichoke with Cheese****

Desserts

White Chocolate Raspberry Cookie, Blackberry Cobbler

Chocolate Oatmeal Delight Bar*

$18.95

Number of * denotes recipe in one of our cookbooks

All of our food is homemade. As much as we would love to accommodate all dietary needs, we are a tea room with limited staff and not a full scale restaurant. Therefore we are unable to accommodate special requests other than vegetarian. We will substitute items without nuts, but we cannot guarantee nut-free foods as we do cook and use nuts in our dishes. There is the possibility of nut dust in all of our items. If you have a nut allergy, we recommend that you bring in your own food and order a pot of tea.

We printed out our menus weekly for a few reasons:

- Our customers often used our menu as a souvenir to take home.
- We published our own cookbooks and we called attention to the specific menu items, which were in our cookbooks. By placing an asterisk next to the menu item, customers knew which recipes were in our cookbooks. This one change in our menu alone doubled the amount of cookbooks we sold at every seating.

We also printed our policies on our menus. Before I opened my tea room, I thought it was "tacky" to have so much clutter and what you can and can't do on the menu. However after a while, I quickly realized why many restaurants put policies on their menu – otherwise you may have a host of other problems.

CHAPTER 15

The Importance of Publishing Your Own Cookbook

If you make all of your own food in your tea room, I can't stress enough the importance of publishing your own cookbook. Not only does this make you more credible but it can also be a huge money maker for your tea room. I started publishing my own cookbook after the first year of opening. I had so many customers who wanted our recipes that it really was to our benefit to create our own cookbook. In the beginning, I just had it printed in spiral bound form at a local printer. Later I ended up starting my own publishing company (ATR Publishing) and printed it through a print on-demand company. We published a cookbook every year with our best recipes. In the beginning it is a lot of work to set it up, but once you do it and have them printed, it makes money for you year after year. Even if you only do one cookbook, it's definitely worth it.

Some tea room owners might be leery of "giving away" their recipes. Don't worry, just because your customers can now make your recipes at home, they won't necessarily do that and it won't be as good as yours. Remember they are coming to tea for the entire experience, not just to buy the recipe. I have found that if you publish a cookbook, your customers will come back even more. They want to see what you are going to make next. In addition, they love the idea of "having" the recipe. I have many customers who don't even cook but still have all of my cookbooks. They also love having you autograph their books. It's a great marketing tool as well. Customers give your books to friends and family, which advertises your tea room. If you do any promotions and networking, your cookbook is a great item to give away.

If you decide to do a cookbook every year like we did, you can have customers "pre-order" their books for a special price. This gives you money up front to print your new book and your customers get a special deal for ordering ahead of time.

When you do set your price for your cookbook, remember this is a special book that they can't get anywhere else, so set your price accordingly.

CHAPTER 16

Tea Room Drama and Handling the Stress of Management

Every work place has its own drama. This is just a part of life. When people work together (or don't work together in some cases) you are bound to have disagreements, hurt feelings, and drama. I have to say, this was my least favorite part of owning and running my tea room. As far as the customers could tell, our tea room ran like clockwork and everyone worked well together. We did our very best to give everyone a wonderful tea experience.

Behind the scenes from my point of view it often looked very different. To tell you the truth, I really hadn't planned on writing a chapter about these problems. However, this was the main stress while I owned my tea room and a large part of the reason I became burned out and closed. I decided that this topic definitely deserved a chapter in the book. It could easily have been an entire book!

Many tea room owners have never managed people before. I myself was one of those people although I didn't know it at the time. I had been a special education teacher and had 3 assistants before I opened my tea room, so I thought I knew about managing staff. I was dead wrong. Managing 15 staff members, all of whom were women of various ages from puberty to menopause with boyfriend issues, abuse issues, divorce issues, sick parents, sick kids and personality differences all had its moments. It's a feat sometimes to keep everyone focused on the job, yet still be sympathetic and understanding. Your staff is your family at work. It's important to communicate effectively. But unlike family, you can do something about unpleasant and unworkable situations. Here are just a few of my personal lessons and guidelines that I learned after owning a tea room for almost 7 years.

- Before I opened, I had been advised in all of my business books, do not hire friends, neighbors and family. I thought at the time, "This won't be a problem for me." However, it was a problem. I'm now a believer! Just don't do it!
- Don't try and be a best friend to your staff. I have an introvert personality. I don't like hurting anyone's

feelings – customers or staff. I learned, you must look out for you and your business first and foremost. Make you and your business the number one priority. Do what works for you, not for anyone else. For example, a staff member may need more hours otherwise they will have to leave to find full time employment elsewhere. If you don't have the money and hours to give, then you will just have to find someone else who can work part-time. It's a tough call sometimes, but you always need to remember your bottom line, otherwise the rest of your employees will not have a job – including you! I have found that it's also a good idea to set up policies so that you don't have to constantly look for answers when questioned about something from a staff member or customer. It's so much easier to say, "Our policy is..."

- You need to pay yourself at least minimum wage from the beginning. You can't work for free even in the beginning. I always paid my staff but didn't always take care of myself. This can quickly lead to burnout. Once I began paying myself even a token amount, I felt differently about the job.

- Don't be afraid to let someone go. You will always find a replacement even if you think you won't. Someone better will come along. You may think you won't find another cook/waitress during the holiday season, but believe me you will or everyone will pull together to make it work. Don't be afraid to fire people who are a bad fit. Hire slowly as they say, and fire quickly.

- "It will get better." This kind of thinking isn't productive when you are talking about staff. No, it probably won't get better unless you do something about it. Problems do not just go away. If you talk with a staff member more than 3 times about a problem, it's probably time to let that person go.
- If someone has a negative attitude and is poisoning the entire mood of the staff, get rid of them. It sounds harsh but negativity is like a cancer and needs to be taken out immediately. You can try and talk to the staff member but if the problem isn't corrected right away, find someone else. Believe it or not, you are doing them as well as yourself a favor by letting them go. The results are usually immediate and positive for everyone.
- Do not talk about staff members with anyone other than your significant other, best friend or coach. If some of your staff members have concerns about other staff members, listen, write the information down, go home and think about it and then take action.
- If you're stressed in managing your staff, get a coach. This helped me tremendously. Having a coach allowed me to see things from a fresh and unbiased perspective. She also gave me suggestions for taking action.
- Make sure you put in time to work "on the business." I thought it was better to be involved with the day to day running of the business for the first 5 years. While it is important to know what is going on, you have to make time to work on your business, otherwise you

won't have a business. When I started setting boundaries such as working from home one day a week, and closing my office door for a few hours a day, I could definitely see results.

- Join a network group. Get out there and find other business owners. Not only will it gain new customers and referrals for you, it will give you access to mentors and people to call when you're feeling alone. Owning a tea room can be very lonely if you let it. Don't let it!

- Delegate! One of the best things I ever did was to divide up my tea room into sections and assign managers to each section. I had a gift shop manager, tea room manager and a kitchen manager. Each staff member reported to his or her manager. That made my life considerably easier. Instead of dealing with all 15 staff and their issues every day, I only had to deal with 3. It allowed me to make decisions rationally without being so personally involved. Staff members first talked to their manager about a problem. Most of the time it was resolved without ever involving me. If someone was sick, they called their manager, not me. This freed up more time for me to work on the business.

- Take care of yourself! Make time for yourself and plan a vacation. I can't stress how important this is. You don't need to take a big trip, but getting away every few months for a few days, gives you a new perspective. Get outside, take a walk, water your flowers and ride your bike. You will come back refreshed, energized and ready for new things.

- Make time for your family. Be careful about always talking about the tea room with your family. Owning a business can consume your life. Your spouse can only take so much of your tea room drama. Be sure and make time for important family events and be available. Your tea room should be able to run without you. If you hire and train the right staff, you will be able to trust your staff to make the right decisions while you are gone.

- You can't please everyone. Although you want to please all of your customers, there will be times when you can't please someone. Just realize this, do your best and move on. If you get a bad review, don't let it ruin your day. The customers that love you often do not write reviews, they will tell you they love you by coming back again and again. It's those customers who really count. So remember those customers and not the one person who left a bad review.

- Don't sweat the small stuff. This lesson probably took the longest for me to learn. I still remember the first weekend I decided to leave the tea room to attend a family wedding. I was nervous about leaving for the first time. On the way to the wedding, one of my staff members called and said that a customer had found a hair in her scone. I was so upset that I wasn't there to deal with the problem. I had my staff give her a new scone and comp her meal. Everything turned out fine. Looking back on that incident, it really was very minor but at the time it seemed so horrible. Realize you are going to make mistakes, how you deal with them is what really counts.

I could go on and on about the lessons I learned from owning a tea room. But then again, every job you have, every experience you have is a lesson in life. Owning a tea room taught me so much about myself and others. It taught me how to appreciate the little things in life and not to take life for granted. It gave me the foundation and confidence to try new things and it reminded me what life is all about – having fun and following your passion! I guess I first had to become a workaholic in order to appreciate the little things in life. So above all else, have fun with your tea room!

ABOUT THE AUTHOR

Amy Lawrence is an example for women who have had many successful careers in life, including teacher and business owner. With a master's degree in Special Education, she taught for 11 years. In 2003 she decided to pursue her passion and opened her tea room, An Afternoon to Remember. Her tea room won many awards including Best Small Tea Room in the U.S. in 2006, KCRA's A-List in 2007, 2008 and 2009, and Sacramento Magazine's Best Tea Room in 2008. In 2009, Amy closed her tea room in order to devote herself full-time to her family and other companies: Afternoon to Remember Fine Tea and Gifts and ATR Publishing. Amy has published nine cookbooks and sold more than 12,000 of them. She is currently working on several new projects, including another tea company called Treasured Leaf.

Also from ATR Publishing

Creating an Afternoon to Remember

A Little of This and a Little of That

Making It Your Own Afternoon to Remember

Tea Time Tidbits and Treats

Drop by for Tea

Master Tea Room Recipes

Order them online at http://www.afternoontoremember.com/

CPSIA information can be obtained
at www.ICGtesting.com
Printed in the USA
BVHW021934280122
627436BV00001B/1

9 780979 617096